Music Minus One Vocals

Big Band Standards
for Females
Vol. 1

Songs by
The Divine One
"Sassy"

mmo

2173

In 1944 Vaughan followed Gillespie and Parker into the new Billy Eckstine Orchestra but, once again, the recording strike was a detriment. Vaughan only recorded one number ("I'll Wait And Pray") during her year with Eckstine.

On Dec. 31, 1944, Sarah Vaughan cut her first four songs as a leader including "East Of The Sun" and a vocal version of Gillespie's "A Night In Tunisia" that was called "Interlude." Five months later, she recorded a few selections with Parker and Gillespie as sidemen. Sassy spent a few months during 1945-46 singing with the John Kirby Sextet and then launched what would be a very successful solo career. Still just 22, she signed with the Musicraft label and recorded mostly jazz-oriented numbers for the next two years, having strong successes with "If You Could See Me Now," "Tenderly" and "It's Magic."

After switching to the Columbia label in 1949, Sarah Vaughan expertly alternated commercial dates with hotter jazz sessions. Her popularity grew on a steady basis throughout the 1950s as she toured constantly, made many television appearances and recorded steadily. She was soon competing with Billie Holiday, Ella Fitzgerald, and Dinah Washington as not only the top female jazz singer but the top female singer in all of music.

During May 18-19, 1950, Vaughan recorded eight particularly rewarding selections while accompanied by an all-star jazz group that included the young Miles Davis in one of his very few sessions with a singer. Among the songs recorded for that project were "Can't Get Out Of This Mood," the beautiful "It Might As Well Be Spring" and George Gershwin's "Nice Work If You Can Get It." Another Columbia session, from Jan. 1953 matched Sassy with a big band and resulted in "Spring Will Be A Little Late This Year."

In 1954, Sassy signed with the Mercury label. Throughout the remainder of the 1950s, her commercial sessions were cut for Mercury while her more swinging dates were made for Mercury's jazz subsidiary Emarcy. One of the most memorable albums was made in Dec. 1954, a date that co-featured the great trumpeter Clifford Brown. Among the songs that they recorded was the definitive version of George Shearing's "Lullaby Of Birdland." Every vocal version made of that song since then has been influenced by Sassy's recording.

Three other numbers in this collection were recorded by Sarah Vaughan later in the 1950s. The saucy "Whatever Lola Wants" was waxed in Mar. 1955 with an orchestra. Erroll Garner's "Misty," a song that because of its wide intervals was once considered almost impossible to sing, was performed effortlessly by Vaughan while backed by the Quincy Jones Orchestra in July 1958. And the touching ballad "Moonlight In Vermont" was recorded with the Count Basie Orchestra in Dec. 1958. The other two songs on this set, Cole Porter's "It's All Right With Me" and Jerome Kern's "Yesterdays," were frequently performed by Vaughan through the years but surprisingly she did not get an opportunity to record them.

During her long career, Sarah Vaughan never really had an off period. Her voice became deeper through the years without losing any of its power, range or brilliance. She toured for decades, drank and smoked, and sometimes got little sleep. Despite that, it did not really matter. Her voice was unaffected and remained wondrous, and her popularity never declined despite the gradual change in the music scene. Sassy remained in her musical prime throughout the 1960s, '70s and even in the 1980s.

Sarah Vaughan remained active up until the end of her life. She passed away from cancer on April 3, 1990 a week after her 66th birthday. While there will never be another singer quite like her, Sassy's recordings are still with us along with the timeless songs that she immortalized.

Scott Yanow, *author of 11 books including The Jazz Singers,*
The Great Jazz Guitarists, Bebop, Jazz On Film and Jazz On Record 1917-76

Big Band Standards
for **Females**, Vol. 1
Songs by The Divine One

CONTENTS

ISBN 978-1-941566-15-2

MMO 2173

Can't Get Out Of This Mood

Frank Loesser and Jimmy McHugh

Whatever Lola Wants

Richard Adler and Jerry Ross

Misty

Erroll Garner and Johnny Burke

Look at me, I'm as help-less as a kit-ten up a tree and I feel like I'm cling-ing to a cloud, I can't___ un-der-stand___ I get mist-y just hold-ing your hand.

Moonlight In Vermont

John Blackburn and Karl Suessdorf

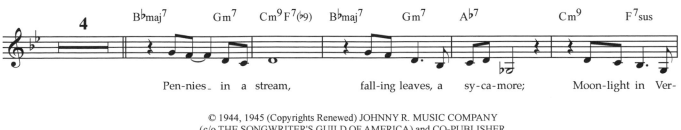

It Might As Well Be Spring

Richard Rodgers and Oscar Hammerstein II

Spring Will Be A Little Late This Year

Frank Loesser

Lullaby Of Birdland

George David Weiss and
George Shearing

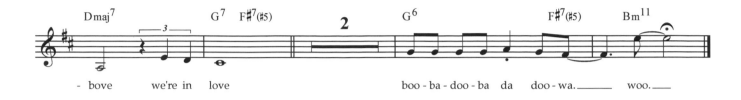

- bove we're in love   boo - ba - doo - ba da doo - wa._____ woo.___

Nice Work If You Can Get It

George Gershwin and Ira Gershwin

Hold - ing hands at mid - night,_ 'neath a star - ry sky;_____ it's

nice work_____ if you can get it, and you can get it if you try._____

Strol - lin' with the one_____ girl, _____ sigh - in' sigh af - ter sigh. It's

nice work_____ if you can get it, and you can get it if you try._____ Just i - mag - ine

some - one_____ wait - ing at the cot - tage door,_____ When two hearts be - come one who could

ask for an - y - thing more? Lov - ing one who loves you,_____ and then tak - ing that vow._____ It's

nice work____ if you can get it, and if you get it,____ won't you tell me how?____

Just i-mag-ine some-one____

wait-ing at the cot-tage door,____ When two hearts be-come one who could ask for an-y-thing

more? Lov-ing one who loves you,____ and then tak-ing that vow.____ It's nice work____ if you can

get it, and if you get it,____ won't you tell me how?____

It's Alright With Me

Cole Porter

It's the wrong time,____ and the wrong place, though your face is____ charm-

- ing it's the wrong face.____ It's not his face,____ but such a charm-ing face,____

free,   well it's al - right,   yes it's al - right

— with me.   You   ba - by don't you

know,   it's al - right with me.

Yesterdays

Jerome Kern and Otto Harbach

Yes - ter-days,   yes - ter-days,

days I knew as hap - py sweet se - quest - ered days.

Ol - den days,   gold - en days,   days of mad ro - mance and

love.   Youth was mine,   truth was mine,

18

Other Great Vocals from Music Minus One

Vol. 1 - Sing the Songs of George & Ira Gershwin......................................MMO 2101
Somebody Loves Me • The Man I Love • Bidin' My Time • Someone To Watch Over Me • I've Got A Crush On You • But Not For Me • S'Wonderful • Fascinatin' Rhythm

Vol. 2 - Sing the Songs of Cole Porter........................MMO 2102
Night And Day • You Do Something To Me • Just One Of Those Things • Begin The Beguine • What Is This Thing Called Love • Let's Do It • Love For Sale • I Get A Kick Out Of You

Vol. 3 - Sing the Songs of Irving Berlin..........................MMO 2103
Cheek To Cheek • Steppin' Out With My Baby • Let's Face The Music And Dance • Change Partners • Let Yourself Go • Say It Isn't So • Isn't This A Lovely Day • This Year's Kisses • Be Careful, It's My Heart

Vol. 4 - Sing the Songs of Harold Arlen......................................MMO 2104
I've Got The World On A String • Down With Love • As Long As I Live • Stormy Weather • I've Got A Right To Sing The Blues • The Blues In The Night • Out Of This World • Come Rain Or Come Shine • My Shining Hour • Hooray For Love

Vol. 5 - Sing More Songs by George & Ira Gershwin, Vol. 2 ....MMO 2105
Of Thee I Sing • Embraceable You • Oh, Lady Be Good • How Long Has This Been Going On? • Summertime • Love Walked In • Nice Work If You Can Get It • I Got Rhythm

Vol. 6 - Sing the Songs of Duke Ellington ....MMO 2106
Do Nothin' Until You Hear From Me • I Got It Bad (And That Ain't Good) • I Let A Song Go Out Of My Heart • It Don't Mean A Thing (If It Ain't Got That Swing) • Mood Indigo • Solitude • Sophisticated Lady • Don't Get Around Much Anymore

Vol. 7 - Sing the Songs of Fats Waller ....MMO 2107
I'm Gonna Sit Right Down And Write Myself A Letter • I've Got A Feeling I'm Falling • Squeeze Me • S'posin' • Two Sleepy People • Ain't Misbehavin' (I'm Savin' My Love For You) • Honeysuckle Rose • I Can't Give You Anything But Love • It's A Sin To Tell A Lie

Vol. 8 - Sing the Songs of Cole Porter, Vol. 2 ....MMO 2108
You're The Top • Easy To Love • Friendship • Anything Goes • Blow, Gabriel, Blow • You're The Top (Jazz Version) • I Get A Kick Out Of You • Anything Goes (Jazz Version)

Vol. 9 - Sing the Songs of Jimmy McHugh ....MMO 2109
It's A Most Unusual Day • You're a Sweetheart • Don't Blame Me • I Feel A Song Coming On • I'm in the Mood for Love • I Can't Give You Anything But Love • I Can't Believe That You're in Love with Me • On the Sunny Side of the Street • I Must Have That Man

Vol. 10 - Sing the Songs of Jerome Kern ....MMO 2110
A Fine Romance • Smoke Gets In Your Eyes • The Last Time I Saw Paris • The Way You Look Tonight • Yesterdays • The Folks Who Live On The Hill • Make Believe • I'm Old Fashioned • All The Things You Are • They Didn't Believe Me

Vol. 11 - Sing the Songs of Johnny Mercer ....MMO 2111
Come Rain or Come Shine • Charade • The Days of Wine and Roses • Dream • I'm Old Fashioned • I Wanna Be Around • Jeepers Creepers • Moon River • One For My Baby

Vol. 12 - Sing the Songs of Johnny Mercer, Vol. 2 ....MMO 2112
The Autumn Leaves • Fools Rush In • I Remember You • My Shining Hour • Skylark • Tangerine • Too Marvelous For Words • Mr. Meadowlark

Vol. 13 - Sing the Songs of Rodgers & Hart ....MMO 2113
I Didn't Know What Time It Was • My Funny Valentine • Nobody's Heart Belongs To Me • A Ship Without A Sail • Dancing On The Ceiling • It Never Entered My Mind • There's A Small Hotel • Where Or When

Vol. 14 - Sing the Songs of Harry Warren..MMO 2114
You'll Never Know • The More I See You • I Wish I Knew • This Is Always • I Had The Craziest Dream • I Only Have Eyes For You • Jeepers Creepers • That's Amore • Serenade In Blue

Music Minus One
50 Executive Boulevard • Elmsford, New York 10523-1325
914-592-1188 • e-mail: info@musicminusone.com
www.musicminusone.com

MMO 2173

ISBN 978-1-941566-15-2